The *Heart* of GOD

True Worship

Dr. Laurita Bledsoe

ISBN 979-8-88616-414-5 (paperback)
ISBN 979-8-88616-415-2 (digital)

Copyright © 2023 by Dr. Laurita Bledsoe

All rights reserved. No part of this publication may be reproduced, distributed, or transmitted in any form or by any means, including photocopying, recording, or other electronic or mechanical methods without the prior written permission of the publisher. For permission requests, solicit the publisher via the address below.

Christian Faith Publishing
832 Park Avenue
Meadville, PA 16335
www.christianfaithpublishing.com

Printed in the United States of America

All quoted scriptures were taken from the Tyndal Life Application Study Bible, KJV. Copyright 1988, 1989, 1990, 1991, 1993, 1996, 2004 by Tyndale House Publishing, Inc., Carol Stream, Illinois 60188. Also used was Thomas Nelson King James Study Bible, Full Color Edition, Copyright 1988, 2013, 2017 by Liberty University, published by Thomas Nelson, Nashville, TN 37214. Words and definitions by the Strong's Exhaustive Concordance of the Bible: Updated and Expanded Edition, Copyright 2007 Hendrickson Publishers Marketing, LLC, P.O. Box 3473, Peabody, MA 0961. Definitions came from the Webster II New Riverside University Dictionary as well as the Merriam-Webster's Collegiate Dictionary Eleventh Edition, Copyright 2003 by Merriam-Webster, Inc.

Note: all references to GOD in the text of the book is capitalized regardless of grammar.

I dedicate this book to those that already have a relationship with the LORD and want to be ignited to go to another level, and for those who desire to develop a relationship with HIM for the very first time. This is for those that want more of HIM and willing to let go more of self. It takes humility, submission and tenacity to break out of the traditions of men and, in some cases, my own traditions in order to cleave to that which pleases the LORD. I dedicate this book to those who are willing to allow the HOLY SPIRIT (not denominationalism, religiosity, tradition, or fear) guide you into all truth and manifest the will of the FATHER. To those that have a willing spirit, an open mind, and the discipline to commit to seeking HIM with your whole heart.

I know you're going to have life-changing experiences in your spiritual journey of intimacy with the LORD, going from faith to faith and glory to glory. Begin to document your journey so it will encourage and strengthen you and others in time of need.

Contents

Acknowledgment ix

Introduction xiii

There's Still a Process 1

The Heart 25

Unity 40

Praise 50

Worship 77

The Glory 91

Decree and Declaration 97

Glossary 99

Acknowledgment

I want to thank the LORD for loving me and placing HIS destiny and purpose on the inside of me. What could I do, or where would I be without HIM? It was destiny for my mom, Evelyn Fields, and my dad, Leroy B. Fields, to be my parents, and I'm grateful. Both of them gave me something different to live by. I love my family, and I'm so appreciative for always having their love and support, no matter what it is that I want to do; and believe me, it's been a lot. They've been there every step of the way.

I have some of the most creative, innovative, and intelligent children, grandchildren, and great grandchildren. I have been blessed to be the matriarch of four generations. To my grandchildren and great grandchildren, you are the joy of my life and the apple of my eye. You are so special to me and know that greatness resides on the inside of you… I love and cherish you so much!

I want to acknowledge my amazing, loving, and faithful children, Miranda, Curtis, and Kia, and their spouses, Charles, Lisa, and Eddie. I've been privileged to experience this scripture, "Her children (grandchildren, great grandchildren) arise and call her blessed" (Proverbs 31:28a). I am so humbled by your love, honor, and care for me that sometimes, it feels unreal. I'm truly blessed to have you as my children, grandchildren and great-grandchildren, and I thank GOD.

I acknowledge the ones who helped hold the family down, my strong, prayerful, and courageous siblings, David, Darnell, Anita, and Velvet. I thank you and love you dearly.

To my good friend, Towanda—gurl, I thank you so much for encouraging me and helping me and making me accountable.

I thank all of the apostles, bishops, elders, pastors, teachers, prophets, evangelists, and prayer warriors who have imparted and undergirded me with prayers during my life's journey and some of my most challenging times; I love and truly appreciate you.

ACKNOWLEDGMENT

I thank you, LORD, for everyone who has ever been a part of my life or influenced it in any kind of way, for I know that all things have worked and are still working together for my good. I thank YOU, LORD, for the abundant life and for all that YOU'VE placed in me to give and allowed me to experience. It's a joy to serve.

Introduction

The only absolutes are the FATHER, the SON, and the HOLY GHOST. What I'm sharing in this book is an aspect of a larger picture based on what the spirit of GOD has revealed to me. This is just one piece of the larger picture with diverse expressions, depths, widths, dimensions, and realms.

I wrote this book because GOD told me to, and it stayed on the shelf for years until an appointed time. Many people come to church, and the praise and worship leader may say it's time for praise and worship. Some may not know what that means or why do you, we have to stand, to clap, or for that matter, to do anything. It may sound elementary to some, but you'll be surprised that some people don't know the difference between praise and worship and what that entails. They just might go along with it or not engage at all.

THE HEART OF GOD TRUE WORSHIP

This book is not written to judge anyone's praise and worship, but it's designed to provoke thought and examine our practices and motives in the area of corporate worship. It's an honor to worship the FATHER in spirit and in truth as well as a choice. So even when I think about going to a place where people are gathered together to pray or worship, I should not go without purpose and intent. Everything GOD has done and will do has purpose, intent, motive, and objective. Why I do what I do is even more important than what I do.

My prayer is that this book will catapult those that praise and worship according to knowledge to another level and those that don't know HIM to new revelations and understanding. Use what you can to advance your personal and corporate worship relationship.

Thus saith the LORD, "Let not the wise man glory in his wisdom, neither let the mighty man glory in his might, let not the rich man glory in his riches. But

xiv

INTRODUCTION

let him that glorieth glory in this, that he understandeth and knoweth *ME*, that I am the LORD which exercise lovingkindness, judgement, and righteousness, in the earth: for in these things I delight, saith the LORD. (Jeremiah 9:23–24)

There's Still a Process

When we come together corporately to praise and worship the LORD, we do not automatically be on the same page or have the same mindset even though we may be in the same place at the same time. There is a lot that comes into play to help bring us together to be on the same spiritual ascension. We praise to worship. Meaning, praise helps to break up and off stuff in and on me to prepare and position me to go from being self-focused to GOD-focused.

When the praise and worship leader invites us to stand, to lift our hands, etc., he or she is trying to provoke and ignite us to join in, which will cause a synergy that will lead to unification. The praise and worship team are not trying to control you but lead you and help you to yield to the guidance of

THE HEART OF GOD TRUE WORSHIP

the HOLY SPIRIT. Praise and worship is for the LORD and not for you. The praise and worship team's job is to invite you to join in, not to entertain you. We all want to experience HIS presence together as HIS body.

"Enter HIS gates with thanksgiving, and into HIS courts with praise; be thankful unto HIM and bless HIS name" (Psalm 100:4). There is still a process.

When we come together corporately, our minds and hearts are not always on entering HIS gates with thanksgiving and into HIS courts with praise. Sometimes it is on, "What I am going to cook for dinner?" or, "Boy, am I hungry." "What am I going to eat when I get out of church?" "I hope church don't be too long today."

Sometimes on Sunday mornings or Saturday nights, we have some of our biggest disagreements with our spouses or significant others that can affect our worship experience. Also, if we are running late or rushing, we can become frustrated, and our minds may be racing when we first come in the church building, and it may take a minute to calm down and to refocus. We can go all week

THERE'S STILL A PROCESS

without misplacing or losing items, but on Sunday mornings on occasions, it can and will happen.

We must intentionally safeguard ourselves because there are many distractions that come to get us off focus. You see, the enemy does not want us to come prepared with intent and purpose to praise the true and living God!

There is a different anointing upon corporate praise and worship than private praise and worship even though your private worship affects how you worship corporately. When I am alone praising and worshipping God, the only person I have to contend with is myself. It is easier to enter in when it is only me versus many people with different personalities, emotions, and mindsets. We come from various walks of life. Therefore, we have different perceptions and views based on our diverse religious, cultural, and ethnic backgrounds.

Some do not even think praise and worship is that important. Some treat praise and worship as a prelude to the preaching of the word only, so they come in late and miss the

3

wonderful opportunity to fellowship corporately with the FATHER. There are some leaders who do not step on to the podium until praise and worship has concluded. There is something HE wants to express to us corporately. As the body of Christ, we must learn that what is important to HIM should be important to us. If we make pleasing HIM the priority, we will begin to work together in partnership with each other and the HOLY SPIRIT, producing the will of the FATHER. When we come together, we must be willing to submit our thoughts to the obedience of CHRIST. Whether a person spends time with GOD will be evident in their ability to engage in praise and worship.

Understand, beloved, there is such an anointing and power that permeates corporate praise and worship as we endeavor to be one sound yet with many voices, one resounding sound but with diverse expressions that comes from a surrendered heart, filled with love and adoration. HE desires the praises of HIS people; HE desires relationship with HIS children. "But THOU art holy, O THOU that inhabitest the praises of Israel" (Psalm 22:3).

THERE'S STILL A PROCESS

In the place where His beloved gathers, He is there. He is everywhere! He has a specific purpose for our coming together. "Draw nigh to God and He will draw nigh to you" (James 4:8a).

Praise and worship are one of the greatest forms of communication with the Lord along with prayer. Prayer, praise, and worship are tools we use to communicate with the Father, but praise and worship is exclusively for and toward Him. Praise and worship have nothing to do with me asking for stuff but has everything to do with me being thankful, grateful, adoring, exalting, and loving Him.

As we begin to think about the goodness of Jesus, His mercy, love, and faithfulness, we become less and less self-focused and become more and more God-focused. We begin to be thankful unto Him and bless His holy name. With a heart of thanksgiving and gratefulness as we think about all that He has brought us through, all He has done, and how much He loves us, we will praise Him. David said, "Because thy lovingkindness is better than life, my lips shall praise thee" (Psalm 63:3). "Let every thing that hath breath praise the

LORD. Praise ye the LORD" (Psalm 150:6). Everything that HE has created praises HIM and gives HIM glory.

There is a process, and we are on our way to worshipping the FATHER in spirit and in truth. JESUS said,

> But the hour cometh, and now is, when the true worshippers shall worship the FATHER in spirit and in truth: for the FATHER seeketh such to worship HIM. GOD is a spirit: and they that worship HIM must worship HIM in spirit and in truth. (John 4:23–24)

When we yield to the HOLY SPIRIT (Spirit of truth), HE will guide us into ascended worship; a yes to HIM and a no to self, complacency, mediocrity, distractions, and compromise. The more I die to self, the more room to be filled with HIS glory and saturated with HIS spirit.

THERE'S STILL A PROCESS

Prepare

Preparedness is key to positioning oneself for the manifestation of GOD's tangible presence. Prepare what? Prepare our minds, hearts, and spirit. We can get our clothes, hair, and whatever else we might need to get ready the night before. Wake up early enough after a good night's rest so that we will not be rushed. During the week, we can spend time on purpose in studying the word of GOD, praying, praising and worshiping, seeking GOD's face. Doing those things will cause us to be in a place of expectancy and faith, waiting for the day when we will all come together in one place on one accord to worship GOD. Wow! When we come together on one accord, we cannot help but experience the tangible presence of GOD, the manifestation of HIS glory, HIS consuming love, and the power of the HOLY GHOST! When we come prepared, it makes it easy for the praise and worship team, so they will not have to try and pump us up, crank us up, or prime us up because we came in the door eager, excited, expecting, and ready! King David said, "Praise waiteth for THEE, O GOD..." (Psalm 65:1a). I can't wait to praise YOU in the congregation of YOUR people. My praise precedes the meeting place because it's already bubbling up in my heart.

Praise and worship are something we can all do together at one time. The HOLY SPIRIT takes the beautiful sounds and lyrics of our voices and blends them all together to create a harmonious symphony that cannot be duplicated. A sound that resonates through eternity to the ears and heart of GOD that causes HIM to respond, "For thus saith the high and lofty One that inhabiteth eternity" (Isaiah 57:15a). As we ascend in worship, heaven will respond and kiss earth. The GOD of mercy and truth will come bearing gifts, salvation, healing, deliverance, comfort, and love to express HIS pleasure toward HIS children. "GOD is not a man, that HE should lie; neither the SON of man, that HE should repent: hath HE said, and shall HE not do it? Or hath HE spoken, and shall HE not make it good?" (Numbers 23:19).

Understand, beloved, GOD is absolute, and HE moves according to HIS divine will

THERE'S STILL A PROCESS

and purpose. "So shall My word be that goeth forth out of My mouth: it shall not return unto Me void, but it shall accomplish that which I please, and it shall prosper in thing whereto I sent it" (Isaiah 55:11). God does nothing useless, empty, and without purpose. When we come together, it should be with purpose and on purpose. Yes, we come to hear the preaching of the word to help us live a Godly life, but that is for us; our worship is for Him. We can enter in boldly before the throne of grace into the holy of holies. "Having therefore, brethren, boldness to enter into the holiest by the blood of Jesus, by a new and living way, which "He hath consecrated for us, through the veil, that is to say, His flesh; and having a high priest over the house of God; let us draw near with a true heart in full assurance of faith, having our hearts sprinkled from an evil conscience, and our bodies washed with pure water" (Hebrews 10:19–22).

We come together for a reason, and it is about God's purpose and plan for our lives. So when we come together knowing that it is the will and plan of God, it shifts our perspective and intention. I have heard many

THE HEART OF GOD TRUE WORSHIP

people say that GOD don't need us—no, HE does not—but HE created us and desires a relationship with us.

Distractions

Let us talk a little bit about distractions in the church. I am not here to judge; I am just bringing information for thought. Why don't we experience miracles, healings, and deliverance like they did every time JESUS came on the scene? JESUS said, "Verily, verily, I say unto you. HE that believeth on Me, the works that I do shall HE do also: and greater works than these shall HE do: because I go unto MY FATHER" (John 14:12). What JESUS did, we should be demonstrating whenever we come together, wherever we go. I have to ask myself as a member of the body of CHRIST, am I doing everything I need to do to please GOD—not accommodate man—in my worship to HIM?

In many ministries today, we send our children to children's church to not only teach them about JESUS but also to minimize disruptions and distractions during the wor-

THERE'S STILL A PROCESS

ship service. So if some ministries have that in place for children, shouldn't it be just as important to minimize distractions from the podium? Actually, in many ways, that which is seen and done on the podium and ushers, etc. sets the tone and precedent for many things that is accepted and done in the church—attire, order, etc.

Much of the compromise has come from the standards of man and not the standards of GOD. The house of GOD was never meant to be the follower of trends but to be the trendsetter. Some of the actions of following the worlds views, standards, styles, etc. has caused us—HIS body—not to be as effective as we ought, and in some cases, confuse the saved and unsaved. JESUS said, "I know thy works, that thou are neither cold nor hot: I would thou wert cold or hot. So then because thou art lukewarm, and neither cold nor hot, I will spue thee out of my mouth" (Revelation 3:15–16).

Just because I can do something, say something, or wear something, it does not mean that I should, or that it is the best thing to do. Apostle Paul said it this way, "All things are lawful for me, but all things are not expedient: all things are lawful for me, but all things edify not" (1 Corinthians 10:12). I am free to do what I want, but I must consider if this is what is pleasing to GOD, especially corporately, and will this cause a problem later on for my sister or brother that may not be spiritually strong. I must seek that which edifies, strengthens, and is the best to do according to the plan and will of GOD. HE knows what is best!

We have so many extremes in churches from strict religious rules to just about no rules at all. The HOLY SPIRIT and the word of GOD, as well as our spiritual leaders and those we can trust for Godly counsel, should be able to be a barometer for us. If what I am saying, doing, or wearing is not pleasing and respectful to GOD, then I should not do it. I remember when I was younger, that the church and everything associated with GOD was so revered, that even when the building was closed, those that cussed would stop cussing when they would walk pass the church. I am saying some things are appropriate and some things are not.

THERE'S STILL A PROCESS

I know that it is not religiously correct to say publicly—even though we may think it, gossip about it—that some things are inappropriate and disrespectful when it comes to how we go before the LORD corporately in praise and worship. In general, we try to be all inclusive and non-offensive, which can cause us not to be definitive and can lead to compromise and tolerance of things that ought not be tolerated. In general, we are trying so hard not to offend people, but what about offending GOD? Speaking the truth from the word of GOD can be an offence to people itself. So do we not speak truth and not offend? Or speak truth and offend? What does GOD say about it?

Even today, a person cannot go and say and do anything before a judge, king, or queen. Some things are conducive for where you are and what you are doing, and some things are not and can be considered disrespectful. For example, you would not dress up in expensive fancy clothes to go and work on a dirty, greasy car engine or wear shorts and a tee shirt with gym shoes, unless requested, to go to the palace to meet the Queen. You can do those things, but it would be considered inappropriate and to meet the Queen, disrespectful.

When we are in court, they say all rise. Unless you are unable to rise, you are going to rise for the Honorable Judge TuTu. Now you may not know Judge TuTu, but you are going to rise and respect the office held by that judge, or you can be held in contempt of court. If we can stand in honor of a natural man or woman we may know nothing about, why is it a struggle for some to stand in honor of the KING of kings and LORD of lords?

These are just examples to say that anything that does not bring honor to GOD and can cause my sister or brother to stumble, I should not do it! If what I am doing, wearing, and saying is a distraction and does not point people to JESUS but brings all the attention to me, then I must reconsider my actions. I may not know what my sister or brother may be struggling with, and I don't want to add to it by being a distraction. I want to do whatever I can to always lead and point them to JESUS.

I have seen—and I'm sure you have, too—worship services that had very little to do with exalting GOD, but everything to do with performing to entertain the people and bring attention to oneself. It is the anointing that breaks the yoke and the spirit of GOD that manifest HIS power and will. We must make pleasing GOD our focus instead of what pleases the people and doing what is the latest thing or trend. We cannot trust our ideas, methods, and styles more than we trust GOD.

There is no young HOLY SPIRIT, old HOLY SPIRIT, or HOLY SPIRIT based on our ethnicity, culture, or style. There is just one HOLY SPIRIT! The HOLY SPIRIT will guide us into all truth, testify of who JESUS is, and manifest the will of the FATHER. JESUS said,

> Howbeit when HE, the Spirit of truth, is come, HE will guide you into all truth: for HE shall not speak of HIMSELF; but whatsoever HE shall hear, that shall HE speak: and HE shall shew you things to come. HE shall glorify ME: for HE shall receive

THE HEART OF GOD TRUE WORSHIP

of mine and shall shew it
unto you. (John 16:13–14)

As the HOLY SPIRIT guides us to worship
in spirit and in truth, HE will speak the heart
of GOD in the midst of HIS people. It is the
truth that can make and set us free. We cannot limit or leave out the guidance and influence of the HOLY SPIRIT. How do we tangibly
experience corporately the intended purpose
of GOD without the spirit of truth, the HOLY
SPIRIT? Truth sets us free to worship. Truth
sets us free to hear revelation from heaven.
Truth sets us spiritually, mentally, physically, relationally, financially, and in many
ways, free. We cannot allow distractions and
compromise to keep us from GOD's will and
purpose from being achieved in our worship
services.

Compromise has caused us, in some
cases in our worship services, not to exceed
pass emotionalism and our natural abilities
and talents. Emotional expression, or the lack
thereof, is not indicative of the anointing and
the power of the HOLY GHOST. Distraction
and compromise can inhibit us, therefore

affecting the flow of the HOLY SPIRIT in our corporate worship. The HOLY SPIRIT will always demonstrate the word of GOD and the power of HIS will. When we come together, HE will be in the midst of us. JESUS said, "For where two or three are gathered together in MY name, there am I in the midst of them" (Matthew 18:20). We, as HIS body, want whatever the intended purpose of the LORD to be accomplished at our gathering together in HIS name. When I come with the knowledge of knowing HE has commissioned this meeting and that HE is going to be there and HE has a plan and purpose in mind, it affects how I come. My intent and motive will be GOD-centered, and I won't be just coming because this is what I ought to do, but I am honored to do.

Faith

"But without faith it is impossible to please HIM, for HE that cometh to GOD must believe that HE is, and that HE is a rewarder of them that diligently seek Him" (Hebrews 11:6).

THE HEART OF GOD TRUE WORSHIP

We cannot please GOD without faith. It is our faith that activates that which GOD has already set in place for us. Our faith has an assignment to agree with and put into action the word, will, and purpose of GOD. Faith without works is dead (James 2:17). Our faith activates that, which is in the spirit realm, to be released at the appointed time. "Through faith we understand that the worlds were framed by the word of GOD, so that things which are seen were not made of things which do appear" (Hebrews 11:3).

Why is it impossible to please HIM? Because we *must* believe that HE is. Believe that HE is:

Sovereign
Almighty
Omniscient: All knowing
Omnipotent: All powerful
Truth
Just
Righteous
Holy
Faithful
Love

THERE'S STILL A PROCESS

Forgiving
Eternal
Immutable

HE changes not! The same yesterday, today, and forever. There are no adequate words or combination of words that can capture the essence of the great "I Am." HE is not a GOD where anyone can go back in the past and say this is the place and moment HE was born and started. No, HE is the eternal ONE, the all existent ONE that dwells in eternity. Believe that HE is your protector, provider, deliverer, healer, and sustainer. HE is the one that brought you through and made a way when there was no way; that healed your body and mended your broken heart. HE is the one that spoke life to you just when you had given up and had lost all hope. HE is the one that put food on your table and blessed you with what you have; your job was just the conduit. It was HIM that opened that door and gave you favor!

Praise HIM with the understanding of who HE is, and why you praise HIM. "For GOD is KING of all the earth: sing ye praises with understanding" (Psalm 47:7). It makes a difference when something is done with understanding, understanding why you are praising Him.

Faith to believe that He is and that He is a rewarder of them that diligently seek Him. The Bible says that if you believe, there are benefits, rewards, blessings attached to you believing that He is. The Bible goes on to say that there is a request God has and that is to seek Him diligently. Diligently: steadily, earnestly, energetic effort; I would say: consistently, purposefully, fervently, passionately. Don't stop. Don't quit. Don't give up, but do it with all of your heart.

As we come together in faith and focus on Him, being led by the Holy Spirit, we will experience the transforming power of the Kingdom of God on earth in us.

The things I talked about does not mean all of those things have to be in place before we have a visitation from God. No! I am suggesting corporately to have a greater move of God, and His intended purpose for His body to be revealed, we can come prepared, expectant, in faith, with focus and diligently.

THERE'S STILL A PROCESS

If we come together and don't give room for the work of the HOLY SPIRIT, but only our agenda, program, and plan, then what do we have? Why are we coming? To please ourselves, or to please GOD?

There are different depths of GOD and levels of revelations of who HE is; deeper realms of intimacy—the place of conception—with GOD.

> For MY thoughts are not your thoughts, neither are your ways MY ways, saith the LORD. For as the heavens are higher than the earth, so are My ways higher than your ways, and My thoughts than your thoughts. (Isaiah 55:8–9)

There are some things that I think I know in the word of GOD and look at that same Scripture a year later and get a whole new revelation. The more I think I know, the more I realize I don't know. I can only enter in, to the degree that I am willing to yield

THE HEART OF GOD TRUE WORSHIP

to the guidance of the HOLY SPIRIT, and HE knows exactly what I can handle. As we submit to the guidance of the HOLY SPIRIT, HE will reveal truth to us according to will of the FATHER.

We must believe that HE is because whatever our inward belief system is, that is what will ultimately manifest. It is not just what you say, but what you believe, that will be made known. "Through faith we understand that the worlds were framed by the word (utterance) of GOD, so that things which are seen were not made of things which do appear" (Hebrews 11:13).

Everything is activated by faith. When we come together in faith and begin with our voices, hearts, and actions extol the true and living GOD, what can't happen in the midst of us? To us and for us, GOD, through faith, formed the worlds. What won't GOD do if we move in faith diligently to worship HIM in spirit and in truth?

GOD is sovereign—supreme authority and power—and can move because HE is and HE wants to. The aforementioned things I have talked about was to make us think about

THERE'S STILL A PROCESS

praise and worship and how we go before Him. This is not a set of rules or regulations for you to adhere to, but information so we can seek to worship HIM according to knowledge with understanding. Remember, it takes humility to grow and learn, and not much effort to remain the same. Unapplied knowledge is just information; it is applied knowledge that empowers us.

I believe as you continue to read this book, the power of the HOLY SPIRIT is going to reveal, refresh, and open the eyes of your understanding. Don't you want to experience the *more*? I know I do. Whatever the *more* is, according to HIS will, I want it. Let's seek HIM together. Let's go from faith to faith and glory to glory.

FATHER, in the name of JESUS, I submit myself to the guidance of the HOLY SPIRIT that HE may teach me how to worship YOU in spirit and in truth. I want all that I do to be in perfect alignment with Your will and purpose. My intent, motive, and focus is to please YOU. I admit, LORD, that I don't always know how to do or what to do, but I know the Spirit of Truth does. So as an act of obedience, I submit my will to the HOLY SPIRIT, so HE may teach me what I need to know. LORD JESUS, reign and rule in and over my life. I thank you for loving me so much and for the privilege to worship you in the beauty of YOUR Holiness.

Whatever the process, LORD, I say yes!

The Heart

The heart is a major component when it comes to worshipping GOD. The condition, position, and substance of the heart is important. I cannot talk about praise and worship without making mention of the heart, the place of ardent expression. "For where your treasure is, there will your heart be also" (Luke 12:34).

Our passions and desires are seated in the center of our hearts. What we value most will be found in the heart. I would say that the heart is where character is formed. "Keep thy heart with all diligence; for out of it are the issues of life" (Proverbs 4:23).

King David said, "Thy word have I hid in my heart that I might not sin against Thee" (Psalm 119:11). In other words, that which I deem valuable—GOD's word—I'm keeping it close to me; for YOUR word is truth, light, and life. FATHER, YOUR word in my heart will lead me to the place where YOU are. YOUR word in my heart will be a source of protection for me. Meditating on YOUR word ignites passion within my heart to give YOU praise. YOUR word declares YOUR greatness and love for YOUR people. FATHER, YOUR word is a keeper and is ever before me. "For Thy word is a lamp (logos) unto my feet and a light (rhema) unto my path" (Psalm 119:105). "Trust in the LORD with all thine heart; and lean not unto thine own understanding. In all thy ways acknowledge HIM, and HE shall direct thy paths" (Proverbs 3:5–6).

It was not that King David was perfect or that HE did everything right. But King David loved GOD, and his hearts' desire was to please Him. David and GOD had a relationship. King David was not ashamed to dance before the LORD with exuberant praise. "And David danced before the LORD with all his might" (2 Samuel 6:14a).

We do not serve a GOD that is lukewarm, mundane, or inconsistent. But HE is consistently faithful, dependable, always the same everyday of every year. The FATHER

THE HEART

gave the very best HE had, HIS only gotten SON; HE held back nothing for you and me. HE deserves our lavish, insatiable, explosive, yielded praise and worship. "As the deer panteth after the water brooks, so my soul panteth after Thee, O GOD" (Psalm 42:1).

GOD's word will reveal what's in our hearts. "For the word of GOD is quick, and powerful, and sharper than any two-edged sword, piercing even to the dividing asunder of soul and spirit, and of joints and marrow, and is a discerner of the thoughts and intents of the heart" (Hebrews 4:12). As we yield to the spirit and the truth of the word, it will transform and realign our hearts to be in right position with GOD. Our hearts in agreement with the word of GOD will provoke us to be on fire for HIM and the things that concern HIM.

Symbolically the heart is a major part of the body that is also hidden. Wherefore the LORD said, "Forasmuch as this people draw near ME with their mouth, and their lips do honor ME, but have removed their heart far from ME, and their fear toward ME is taught by the precept of men" (Isaiah 29:13) Mark

THE HEART OF GOD TRUE WORSHIP

7:6–7). "What I do on the outside, my works can be seen, but my motive and intent are hidden. Why I do what I do is found in the heart. What is done behind closed doors, in the dark, when nobody else can see, hear or know…reveals more about what's in my heart than the things that can be seen.

Listen… What do you hear? What do you think about the most? What are your passions, appetites, desires, and tendencies? Where does the word marinate? Where do you ponder the word? I submit to you to consider; it's the heart. "For as HE thinketh in his heart, so is he" (Proverbs 23:7a). Our hearts should be on the things of the LORD.

> But his delight is in the law of the LORD; and in HIS law doth HE meditate day and night. And HE shall be like a tree planted by the rivers of waters, that bringeth forth his fruit in his season; his leaf also shall not wither; and whatsoever HE doeth shall prosper. (Psalm 1:2–3)

THE HEART

GOD is more interested in what's on the inside of us than that which is external. Don't get me wrong, faith without works is dead (James 2:17). What's on the inside of us can affect every aspect of our lives. Inwardly we must be surrendered to the guidance of the HOLY SPIRIT and submitted to the LORDSHIP of JESUS CHRIST. The FATHER's desire is that we be like HIM. Inwardly obedient to HIS word and will, outwardly displaying it in love, servitude, and in great demonstration of HIS power.

Let's examine the natural heart symbolically to bring clarity to what's being said about the spiritual heart. What are some of the functions of the heart? The heart is:

1. Made of muscles/chambers
2. Pumps blood
3. The place of distribution of blood/oxygen
4. The heart is necessary to sustain life

If the heart is not healthy, it can malfunction and affect how blood and oxygen is distributed throughout the body. The heart can have a blockage or weak muscles. Whatever the reason for the unhealthy heart, it can ultimately affect the entire body. We cannot live without a functioning heart.

If the blood that the heart pumps is tainted, it can infect every place the blood goes. Beloved, that is the same as if what is in our spiritual hearts is not of GOD. As a result of what's in our hearts, we will begin to speak it, and eventually exhibit outwardly what we inwardly think and feel. If what is in our hearts is tainted, it can poison the mind and distort vision. It can influence how we perceive things; how we hear, what we speak, and how we process information.

Listed are some potential blockages and hinderances that may be in the heart that can affect one's praise and worship:

Unbelief, pride, disobedience, unforgiveness, guilt/shame, unforgiveness, religiosity (rituals/rigidity), spectatorship, distraction, familiarity, complacency, idolatry, wrong attitude, lack of sensitivity to the HOLY SPIRIT,

THE HEART

rebellion, discord/lack of unity, lack of love, dryness/barrenness, sin, lack of vision.

> Keep thy heart with all diligence; for out of it are the issues of life. (Proverbs 4:23)

> For out of the abundance of the heart the mouth speaketh. A good man out of the good treasure of the heart bringeth forth good things; and an evil man out of the evil treasure bringeth forth evil things. (Matthew 12:34c–35)

Whatever is harbored in our hearts is what will be heard and seen in one way or another. "Out of the same mouth proceeded blessing and cursing. My brethren, these things ought not so to be" (James 3:10).

> But things which proceed out of the mouth come

THE HEART OF GOD TRUE WORSHIP

> forth from the heart; and
> they defile the man. For
> out of the heart proceed evil
> thoughts, murders, adul-
> teries, fornications, thefts,
> false witness, blasphemies.
> (Matthew 15:18–19)

Some of the things mentioned as coming forth from the heart are also listed as the works of the flesh (Galatians 5:19–21).

> Create in me a clean
> heart, O GOD; and renew
> a right spirit within me.
> (Psalm 51:10)

The position (attitude) and condition of the heart affects our worship. How do I keep my spiritual heart healthy, free of blockages, and in good condition? One way is by meditating on the word of GOD. Think on those things that produce life and godliness. "But as HE which hath called you is holy, so be ye holy in all manner of conversation; because it is written, Be ye holy; for I am holy" (I Peter

THE HEART

1:15–16). Practice and apply the word of GOD until it gets into your heart and assimilates into every part of your existence.

Protect your eye gate, ear gate, and what you receive into your heart. All sin basically enters in through the lust of the eyes, the lust of the flesh, and the pride of life (1 John 2:16). Be careful about what you allow yourself to agree with and your mouth to speak and your heart to ponder on and your mind to imagine. Guard yourself! Put on the whole amour of GOD (Ephesians 6:14–18).

> Finally, brethren, whatsoever things are true, whatsoever things are honest, whatsoever things are just, whatsoever things are pure, whatsoever things are lovely, whatsoever things are of a good report; if there be any virtue, and if there be any praise, think on these things. (Philippians 4:8)

THE HEART OF GOD TRUE WORSHIP

As we meditate on the word of God and regurgitate it, our spiritual heart muscles will get stronger and stronger. We're doing exercise! Eat the word of God, it's uhm, uhm good! "How sweet are Thy words unto my taste! yea, sweeter than honey to my mouth!" (Psalm 119:103).

Apostle Paul said,

> Rejoice in the Lord always: and again I say, Rejoice. Let your moderation be known unto all men. The Lord is at hand. Be careful for nothing; but in everything by prayer and supplication with thanksgiving let your request be known unto God. And the peace of God, which passeth all understanding, shall keep your hearts and minds through Christ Jesus. (Philippians 4:4–7)

THE HEART

I wrote all of that so that you can see what will keep your heart and mind. Apostle Paul says, "Rejoice, declare to everyone that the LORD is at hand. Make your prayers and supplications along with thanksgiving, and the peace of GOD that we just cannot understand will keep our hearts and minds through our LORD and Savior JESUS CHRIST."

Listed below are some other suggestions on how we can keep our heart flowing healthy and unclogged:

Faith
Meditate on the word
Confession of sin
A repented heart
Make prayer, praise and worship a state of being
Submit to the guidance of the HOLY SPIRIT
Obey the word and will of GOD
Trust and depend on the LORD
Walk in love
Walk in humility
Exercise the fruit of the HOLY SPIRIT

THE HEART OF GOD TRUE WORSHIP

Have an attitude of thankfulness and gratefulness
Endeavor to walk in unity with the brethren
Forgive
Correct alignment with GOD and godly authority

Whatever or whomever we allow to sit at the helm of our hearts, that is what we'll worship. Allow JESUS to take a seat on the throne of your heart; the place of passion and ardent love. JESUS said unto him, "Thou shalt love the LORD thy GOD with all thy heart, and with all thy soul, and with all thy mind. This is the first and great commandment" (Matthew 22:37–38). "Praise ye the LORD, I will praise the LORD with my whole heart, in the assembly of the upright, and in the congregation" (Psalm 111:11). All that is within us, we will love and praise the LORD!

JESUS said, "For where your treasure is, there will your heart be also" (Matthew 12:34).

THE HEART

One day, me and the LORD were talking, and HE asked me, "Do you remember when you were in love?"

And I said, "Yes."

HE then asked me, "How did you feel? What did you do?"

Of course, you know that was a rhetorical question, because HE already knew the answers. I knew then that it was school time and there was something HE wanted to reveal to me.

I said, "When I was in love, I thought about him a lot, periodically, through the day. It was like he was a part of me that I could feel him even when he was not around. I would get excited at the thought of seeing him or anticipating his call. Just being around him made me feel warm, safe, and secure. I would think of ways to please him like preparing his favorite food, buying him something, things that would make him laugh and put a smile on his face."

Now what the LORD was causing me to see was this is how I feel about a natural man. How much more should I desire to be in HIS presence? How much more should I long to

THE HEART OF GOD TRUE WORSHIP

please HIM, to be aware of HIM. The FATHER showed this to me so that I could see how much value sometimes I place on others and things more than I do HIM.

HE said, "What if MY children were excited about ME, and stayed in a place of anticipation of seeing ME...of hearing MY voice...of spending quality time with ME? What would happen if MY children sought ME with all of their heart to please ME?"

I began to think about what the LORD was saying, and I could see it like a movie. I said to HIM, "LORD, I can't imagine being without YOU. I've never known a love like YOUR love, LORD. A love that never fails, that can heal the deepest hurt. LORD, I said YOU know all about me... Every thought, intent, motive...everything I've ever done and said, and YOU still love me anyway. What kind of love is this?"

HE made me think...how much effort does it take me to do what I do? What does it cost me? "Give ME more than what's easy to give; more than what's familiar to you." HE is saying to me and you to reach higher, go deeper, stay longer, be hungry for HIM. The

THE HEART

LORD was saying, "Go pass normality, familiarity, comfortability…to that secret place, the place where you can sup with ME and I with you." HE was and is saying to us, there is more, more of ME, more I want you to see… come…come… I say come.

I got it! I see it! I'm determined to praise and worship HIM in the way and to the extent that is pleasing to HIM. What about you? At this moment begin to meditate on HIM and set your heart to go deeper… Write down what you hear and see as the Spirit of GOD begins to minister to you as you set your heart on the LORD.

"My soul longeth, yea, even fainteth for the courts of the LORD: my heart and flesh crieth out for the Living GOD" (Psalm 84:2).

"I will love Thee, O LORD, my strength" (Psalm 18:1).

Unity

Unity: The quality or state of being or being made one: oneness; concord, harmony; continuity without change.

Unite: To put or join together so as to make one; to join by a legal or moral bond.

Union: An act or instance of uniting two or more things into one.

Synergy: The interaction or cooperation of two or more people, organizations, substances, or other agents to produce a combine effect greater than the sum of their separate effects; the increased effectiveness that results when two or more people or businesses work together.

We cannot have unity as a collective group without humility. It takes us submitting to each other as we submit to the guidance of the HOLY SPIRIT.

UNITY

One of the main things our adversary wants to do is to keep us divided. For he knows that if we come not only to the revelation of what comes from being unified but also pursue unity...it's over for him.

There is so much power and strength that comes from being one. The enemy fights marriages tooth and nail because he hates the power of oneness that comes from GOD's ordained purpose. JESUS said, "Again I say unto you; That if two of you shall agree on earth as touching anything that they shall ask, it shall be done for them of MY FATHER which is in heaven" (Matthew 18:19). Being in the place of agreement with each other and the will of the FATHER positions us to see, be, and do the exceeding abundant more than we can ask or think thing! There are no limits other than those set by the Almighty. One can chase a thousand and two can put ten thousand to flight (Deuteronomy 32:30, Joshua 23:10).

In Genesis, chapter 11, it talks about the Tower of Babel. "And the whole earth was of one language, and one speech" (Genesis 11:1). Read verses one to nine for yourself. So the people decided to build a tower that would reach to heaven. And the LORD said, "Behold, the people is one, and they have all one language; and this they begin to do: and now nothing will be restrained from them, which they have imagined to do" (Genesis 11:6). The LORD was saying they will do it! They were of one language and one mind and unified, there was nothing they could not do. So GOD confounded them by changing their language, and that changed the entire course of things.

Beloved, can you see what kind of relationship we can have, being unified as the body of CHRIST with one voice and heart; not to reach heaven for our own glory and fame but to please the FATHER and fulfill HIS purpose for our lives.

Unity is HIS desire that we, being many members of HIS body, flow and operate as one. That we, being comprised of many units, function in the capacity that each one of us were created yet in harmonious continuity.

When we worship in unity, it creates a sound. It's not a fragmented sound but a synergistic flow that apprehends and alters the atmosphere. For example, an experienced

UNITY

mechanic can listen to a car engine and tell if something is not connecting or firing correctly. There's a sound. There's a rhythm. When fans come together at a sports event and begin to chant and do the wave collectively, it charges the atmosphere, and it's electrifying. The actions of the fans are contagious, and excitement is magnified. Expectations emits in the air, and the players respond with heighten enthusiasm!

Beloved, do you see it? The combination of all of GOD's children being in one place, with one voice, with one purpose to praise the LORD ecstatically! Praising HIM that way will cause a GODly response.

Praising and worshipping the LORD in unity, not only creates a sound, a synergistic flow, but it also infiltrates and rearranges the atmosphere, emitting an aroma and producing a habitation suitable for the LORD to dwell in.

When the day of Pentecost fully came, they were with one accord in one place and suddenly there came a sound from heaven as a mighty, rushing wind, and they were filled with the HOLY GHOST and spoke in other

THE HEART OF GOD TRUE WORSHIP

tongues as the SPIRIT gave them utterance (Acts 2:1–4).

Expect something to happen when we come together in unity. Every place in the Bible when the people of GOD came together in unity, there was a response from heaven.

Let's look at what happened on the day of Pentecost that created this life changing encounter. It happened first of all because JESUS said it would (Acts 1:5).

Pentecost fully came. It was celebrated fifty days after Passover. It was called the Feast of the Weeks or Feast of the Harvest.

It was a festival of thanksgiving for the harvested crops. It was done annually at a set time. There was preparation for the celebration. There was an attitude of thankfulness and gratefulness to GOD that was noised in the atmosphere.

Those that were in the upper room were in one place on one accord with a mindset of excitement and anticipation, and they were previously in prayer. Whenever GOD calls a meeting, it is *never* unfruitful or empty, but always with divine purpose and intent. HE knows what HE wants out of every time we

44

UNITY

come together, for we were made for His good pleasure. "Thou art worthy, O Lord, to receive glory and honor and power; for Thou hast created all things, and for Thy pleasure they are and were created" (Revelation 4:11).

His desire is always the best for us, and He knows what is best for us. "Fear not, little flock; for it is your Father's good pleasure to give you the kingdom" (Luke 12:32). "And the glory which Thou gavest Me I have given them: that they may be one even as We are one" (John 17:22).

Even when the Lord sent the disciples out, He did not send them out alone. Throughout the word of God, He's showing us that it's not about the me, myself, and I, but more times than not, it's about a *we* and *us*, about His body, about His beloved. Individuals make up the body, and there are times that it will be about you but still in connection with your divine purpose and destiny as it relates to others.

As we flow in unity in this dimension, not only will we be changed but also our families, communities, nations, and spheres. The glory of God will be revealed.

THE HEART OF GOD TRUE WORSHIP

There's such power in being unified that the enemy is working overtime trying to get us disputing on this or that, or questioning God; Did you really say? The enemy tries to get us distracted or out of order by any means necessary, if only for a little while. The enemies' tactics may delay us for a moment. However, there's an expected end that the Lord has for us. "For I know the thoughts that I think toward you, saith the Lord, thoughts of peace, and not of evil, to give you an expected end" (Jeremiah 29:11).

We belong to Him and none can take us from Him. Jesus said, "My Father, which gave them Me, is greater than all; and no man is able to pluck them out of My FATHER's hand. I and My Father are one" (John 10:29–30).

"But ye are a chosen generation, a royal priesthood, a holy nation, a peculiar people; that ye should shew forth the praises of Him who hath called you out of darkness into His marvelous light." (1 Peter 2:9).

We have this prestigious position God has placed us in. The honor to be able to go

UNITY

before His throne; the privilege to give Him exalted praise and intimate worship.

The Holy Spirit, as the symphonic conductor, takes many voices and creates one sound. Many cultures and ethnicities birth one people in melodious, synergistic worship. We are one body, and just as each part of our natural bodies flows in rhythmic harmony with each other to create a systematic organism, so is the body of Christ. Apostle Paul said, "Fulfill ye my joy, that ye be like minded, having the same love, being one accord of one mind" (Philippians 2:2).

Our praise and worship are exclusively for and toward Him. We know that He said He is in the midst of us as we seek His face as one. He wants us to be one as He and the Father are one.

> And now I am no more
> in the world, but these are
> in the world, and I come to
> Thee. Holy Father, keep
> through thine own name
> those whom Thou hast

THE HEART OF GOD TRUE WORSHIP

given ME, that they may be
one, as WE are. (John 17:11)

GOD loves us so much, and HE looks
forward to the times we come together intentionally to commune with HIM. In my mind, it reminds me of an intimate dinner: a sweet aroma fills the room, the candles are lit, and the table is spread, beautifully set waiting for the guest of honor to enter the room. As we come together in anticipation of HIS presence, we set the tone, the ambiance for the guest of honor, the KING of Glory!

One of HIS delights is when HIS children come to HIM in adoration and love. How pleasant it is when our children are united and express their love and respect towards us as parents. Doesn't it feel good? When our children are obedient and appreciative, let's be honest, there's nothing we wouldn't do for them. Beloved, if we feel that way about our children, can you imagine what the LORD feels about us? When we come in unity to worship HIM, it pleases HIM and who HE is will begin to illuminate in the midst of us and the treasures of heaven will be released; unin-

UNITY

terrupted, unrestricted, communion with the FATHER.

"There is neither Jew nor Greek, there is neither bond nor free, there is neither male nor female: for ye are all one in CHRIST JESUS" (Galatians 3:28).

Praise

What does it mean to praise GOD? Praise means: to glorify/ to speak with approval or admiration/to celebrate, to rave, to boast, value, merit, extol, magnify,…

What is ascendant praise? (intentional)

Moving forward: rising, directed upward, superior, to succeed to, to occupy.

Who can praise GOD?

Everything that has breath or that GOD has created can praise the LORD! In Psalm 148, the anonymous author declares that all creation should praise the LORD: angles, sun, moon, stars, mountains, hills, beasts, creeping things, young and old men, women, children, kings, princes, judges, etc.; Let everything that have breath praise the LORD!

PRAISE

The Bible says in Psalm 100:4 that we should, "Enter into His gates with thanksgiving, and into His courts with praise: be thankful unto Him and bless His name." According to the word of God, how should we enter? With thanksgiving, which describes the kind of attitude we should have when we come to the house of the Lord or wherever the children of the Most High are gathering. There is an outward demonstration of our thankfulness and gratitude that's expressed in our various forms of praise. When we examine this scripture, we see a progression, so as it is with praise and worship.

Praise and worship should cause us to ascend from where we are by the guidance of the Holy Spirit to the realm of the will and purpose of God. This progression is expressed by the outer court (our body), the inner court (souls) and the holy of holies (our spirits).

I want to use the analogy of an airplane. When we go to catch our plane, we enter into a gate—His gates with thanksgiving. When we get on the plane, we are all in there together. There are not some on the outside on the wings of the plane nor on its roof, but

THE HEART OF GOD TRUE WORSHIP

we're all in there together. As the plane takes off, it goes down the runway—courts with praise—and it begins to ascend—bless His holy name—to the delegated altitude of the pilot—HOLY SPIRIT. We were never meant to stay at the gate, nor sit at the runway, but to ascend to the place the LORD would have us to go.

King David said, "Praise waiteth for THEE, O GOD, in Sion" (Psalm 65:1a). In other words, you don't have to pump me, prime me, persuade me, or provoke me; I'm ready. Everything inside of me is giving YOU glory even before the minstrel strikes a chord... I can't wait to praise THEE!

LORD, I've been thinking about YOU all day, all week. I can't wait to praise You! My praise precedes me! I'm not waiting for the musicians or singers, but, LORD, when I think about YOUR goodness and all that YOU'VE done for me, my soul cries out Hallelujah! "Bless the LORD, O my soul: and all that is within me, bless His holy name" (Psalm 103:10). Every part of me—mind, body, soul—engages, purposefully, intentionally, transforming into an instrument, a vessel of praise. There's no one

PRAISE

that can praise HIM like I can for what HE has done for me.

Praise is not predicated upon our feelings, emotions, or circumstances, but it is a command, an act of our will! It does not matter about your economic or academic status. Whether you are an introvert or extravert. Praise HIM!

I remember one time, the LORD asked me, "If you did not feel ME, could you still praise ME?" To tell you the truth, I had to stop and think about what HE had just asked me... Then I said to HIM, "Yes, LORD. I could." Then I began to say to HIM, "LORD, we have history together and at every turn and situation in my life, YOU were there. Through the ups and downs and not knowing which way to go, YOU were there. When I can't depend on anything else, I can Always depend on YOU. I went on to say, because LORD YOU are faithful and whether I feel YOU or not does not nullify who YOU are and what YOU have done. Just because someone doesn't believe in YOU, does not mean that YOU are not real."

When we examine what happens in praise, you will see that some of the dynamics

THE HEART OF GOD TRUE WORSHIP

are a little different than worship. In praise, there's normally activity, movement, and noise. In Psalm 100:1, it says, "Make a joyful noise unto the LORD, all ye lands." That verse in the Old Testament is repeated in other chapters. Make a joyful noise in Hebrew is the word *ru'wa* which figuratively means to split the ears with sound. Before many of the wars that were fought in the Bible, they would send forth the worshippers.

Second Chronicles 20 tells of how Jehoshaphat defeated Moab and Ammon. Moab and Ammon were going to battle against Jehoshaphat. Jehoshaphat was afraid and sought the LORD and called a fast throughout Judea. This unified submission set the tone for GOD to move. In verse 17, GOD said,

> Ye shall not need to fight in this battle: set yourselves, stand still, and see the salvation of the LORD with you, O Judah and Jerusalem: fear not, nor be dismayed; tomorrow go out against

PRAISE

them: for the LORD will be
with you.

Then they worshipped GOD. They rose
up early and Jehoshaphat appointed singers unto the LORD; that they should praise
the beauty of HIS holiness, as the worshippers went out before the army (v. 22). When
they began to sing and to praise, the LORD
set ambushes against the children of Ammon
and Moab, and GOD caused them to destroy
each other...none escaped. I don't even know
if Moab and Ammon could even identify the
words of the singers, but I know they heard
the thunderous sound of praise that preceded
them like a mighty hammer, and it caused the
atmosphere to work in concert with the plan
of GOD to execute judgement against the enemies of Judah and Jerusalem! The riches were
so great; it took them three days to gather the
spoils.

"Let GOD arise and HIS enemies be
scattered" (Psalm 68:1a). Praise is a mighty
weapon of war. That's why praise cannot be
handled as if it's not important or taken for
granted as this is just something we do as a

THE HEART OF GOD TRUE WORSHIP

part of the program or as an afterthought. No! No! No! We were created to praise HIM before we ever received titles, degrees, wealth, or notoriety. We were created to commune, fellowship, worship, and honor HIM. GOD inhabits (lives/dwells in) the praises of HIS people (Psalm 22:3).

In Psalm 8:4, David says, "Out of the mouth of babes and sucklings hast THOU ordained (established) strength because of thine enemies, that thou mightiest still (immobilize) the enemy and the avenger." JESUS says it this way in Matthew 21:16, "Yeah, have ye never read, out of the mouth of babes and sucklings THOU hast perfected praise." As we praise GOD, our praise will ignite, arrest and transform the atmosphere and render our enemies helpless as well as silence our flesh. Our praise binds the enemy not only in the earthly realm but also in the heavens. JESUS said to Peter,

> And I will give unto thee the keys of the Kingdom of Heaven: and whatsoever thou shalt bind on earth

PRAISE

shall be bound in heaven: and whatsoever thou shalt loose on earth shall be loosed in heaven. (Matthew 16:19)

Our praise will shut the enemy and the avenger down! Our prayer, praise, and worship are keys.

When we praise God, and lift our hands as an act of surrender, saying, "Lord here we are, just as we are, take us to a place of humility, submission into repentance. When we stand in the glory of God, in His presence, we can't help but bow and realize that our best is as filthy rags in His brilliance, holiness, magnificence and power!

Where do we praise God?

Psalm 149:1, "Praise ye the Lord. Sing unto the Lord a new song, and his praise in the congregation of saints." Psalm 150:1, "Praise ye the Lord. Praise God in His sanctuary: praise Him in the firmament of His power." Hebrews 2:12, "Saying, I will declare thy name unto my brethren, in the midst of

THE HEART OF GOD TRUE WORSHIP

the church will I sing praise unto THEE." In Acts 16:25–34, it talks about how Paul and Silas were bound and in prison and prayed and praised GOD at midnight. As a result of Paul and Silas praying and praising, the earth quaked, the foundation of the prison was shaken, the prison doors swung open, and everyone's bands were loosed.

Beloved, the prison and bands can represent bondages and strongholds we may have in our own lives. Just as there was breakthrough and freedom that happened as a result of their actions and faith in GOD, the same thing can happen for us. HE will respond to our cry as we sincerely praise HIM. For HE has never, ever failed us yet! "I sought the LORD and HE heard me, and delivered me from all my fears" (Psalm 34:4).

We can praise GOD anywhere. Isn't that a wonderful thing? One place I find myself praising the LORD a lot is when I'm by myself, driving in the car, and having a good old time. I remember how my mom would hum and sing spiritual songs while she was cooking in the kitchen. No wonder her food was so delicious. I find myself humming and mak-

58

PRAISE

ing melodies in my heart all through the day.
Ephesians 5:19–20,

> Speaking to yourselves in psalms and hymns and spiritual songs, singing and making melody in your heart unto the LORD; giving thanks always for all things unto GOD and the FATHER in the name of our LORD, JESUS CHRIST.

There are no limits as to where you can praise HIM. So if you find yourself being restricted as in where you can praise HIM, I encourage you…to take the limits off!

When do we praise?

"By HIM let us therefore offer the sacrifice of praise to GOD continually, that is, the fruit of our lips giving thanks to HIS name" (Hebrews 13:5). Sometimes when we're in a hard place, we must press our way to praise HIM because we know when we praise HIM,

THE HEART OF GOD TRUE WORSHIP

not only will we feel better, but it also shifts our focus from our problems to the problem solver, and HE is faithful to deliver and will not fail!

Many people have said what the enemy is after. I think one of the main things he is after is our voice. I believe he is saying, "If I can just cause enough issues in his/her life, they will stop praising HIM and causing havoc in my kingdom. Then once their voice begins to be silent, I can get them off by themselves and bombard them with lies of defeat."

The power of the sound of praise out of the believer's mouth causes the enemy to be ineffective. GOD gave us the example of speaking throughout chapter 1 in the book of Genesis where GOD spoke. GOD is so bad, HE could've just thought it into existence, but no; HE spoke it! So let's declare HIS goodness out of our mouths and watch the victory of the LORD! There is power in our voices. When we begin to declare who HE is, it causes us, and the atmosphere, to become infused with the power and strength of GOD.

As we look up, we can begin to see our help coming. "I will look unto the hills, from

60

PRAISE

whence cometh my help. My help cometh from the LORD, which made heaven and earth" (Psalm 121:1–2). "THOU art my hiding place; THOU shalt preserve me from trouble; THOU shalt compass me about with songs of deliverance" (Psalm 32:7). "By THEE have I been holden up from the womb: THOU are HE that took me out of my mother's bowels: my praise shall be continually of THEE" (Psalm 71:6).

GOD spoke to the prophet Jeremiah and said, "Before I formed thee in the belly I knew thee." (Jeremiah 1:5a). That Scripture speaks of a place of intimacy.

Psalm 34:1, "I will bless the LORD at all times: HIS praise shall continually be in my mouth." We bless HIS name continually; all of the time! No matter what. In the good times, in the bad times, in the times when I can't seem to hear GOD speaking, I will bless HIS name. I will praise HIM even though I don't feel like it.

It is interesting that some of us come to the house of the LORD and are not participators but sit as spectators, mouths closed, hands clinched, and some even on their phones.

This scripture says we're to bless HIM, glorify HIM, extol HIM nonstop with our mouths. What makes it puzzling is that most of us drove to church in some kind of vehicle. We walked into the building. We live in a house/apartment, and we can think and talk.

GOD blesses us with the ability to get wealth. Deuteronomy 8:18ab says, "But thou shalt remember the LORD thy GOD: for it is HE that giveth thee power to get wealth." It is HE that blesses us to see another day with health and strength and all the other needs and wants that we have. It is not of our own strength and abilities that we are able to do these things, but it is the love, grace, and mercy of our eternal GOD. We should make HIS praise resound, so that the earth would shake and the buildings sway and the trees wave their hands! "Sing forth the honor of HIS name: make HIS praise glorious" (Psalm 66:2).

I don't understand why one would take the time to get up, take care of their hygiene, get dressed, and drive or walk to church and then doesn't participate. Listen, if this is you, make up your mind to choose never to miss

PRAISE

out on the ordained, blessed opportunity to engage in corporate praise and worship.

We praise HIM intentionally with purpose, not just because we need a breakthrough but because HE's so worthy, HE is GOD. GOD is so awesome, even though the praise and worship is for HIM, HE blesses us, heals us, delivers us, and saves us right in the midst of our praise. What an indescribable, wonderful, sovereign GOD we serve! HE actually rewards us (if I can say that) for giving HIM what is due HIS name. Wow!

The FATHER is constantly displaying HIS love for us and asking, wooing us to come and spend time with HIM. There's no way if we praise HIM continually would we be depressed, sad, or in despair because exalting HIM causes our view of our situation to change. It changes us. As we lift up the name of JESUS, our problems diminish in the light of HIS power and strength. HE is our fortress, battle axe, refuge, protector, and keeper. I realize every day that I live, that I can't keep myself, that it is GOD who is my keeper. Every breath that I take it is because of HIM.

THE HEART OF GOD TRUE WORSHIP

I'm alive because He has destined me to live. Lord, I give You praise!

How do we praise Him?

"I will praise Thee with my whole heart: before the gods will I sing praise unto Thee" (Psalm 138:1). We praise Him with our voices, hands, in dance with all kinds of instruments, with anything and everything, we give Him praise! "O clap your hands, all ye people; shout unto God with the voice of triumph" (Psalm 47:1). "Let them praise His name in the dance: let them sing praises unto Him with the timbrel and harp" (Psalm 149:3).

In Psalm 150, it speaks of praising God for His mighty acts and according to His excellent greatness. Praising Him with the trumpet, psaltery, harp, timbrel, dance, stringed instruments, organs, loud cymbals, high sounding cymbals. "Let everything that hath breath praise the Lord" (Psalm 150:6). "One generation shall praise Thy works to another, and shall declare Thy mighty acts" (Psalm 145:4). This is exciting, generational

PRAISE

praise! We're not only to spread the gospel, but we're also to spread the praise!

JESUS said, "Let your light so shine before men, that they may see your good works, and glorify your FATHER which is in heaven" (Matthew 5:16). Everything that we do should cause people to want to know the GOD that we serve, that we worship. In Luke 19:37–38, all the disciples began to rejoice and praise GOD with a loud voice for HIS mighty works and bless HIM.

In verse 39, the Pharisees told JESUS to rebuke HIS disciples. In other words, shut them up! IN VERSE 40, JESUS replied, "I tell you that, if these should hold their peace, the stones would immediately cry out." JESUS was saying if the disciples did not worship HIM, then creation (stones/rocks) would!

Why do we praise GOD?

There are so many reasons why we should praise the LORD, but the first thing I can think of is just because HE is GOD, our creator. What can I say, HE's our: provider, protector, deliverer, healer, way maker, redeemer,

THE HEART OF GOD TRUE WORSHIP

restorer, reconciler, peace, joy, hope, intercessor, revelator, friend, refuge, strength; HE loves us with an everlasting love. HE is our creator and blesser, (Genesis 2:27–28). HE is good (Psalm 136:1b) HE is merciful (Psalm 103:10). "HE hath not dealt with us after our sins; nor rewarded us according to our iniquities." HE's forgiving, "If we confess our sins, HE is faithful and just to forgive us our sins, and to cleanse us from all unrighteousness" (1 John 4:16). HE is love, GOD so loved the world, that HE gave the very best that HE had, HIS only begotten SON; HE held back nothing (John 3:16). HE is dependable and faithful: HE cannot lie (Numbers 23:19), HE does not change (Malachi 3:6) (Hebrews 13:8).

I could go on and on. There's nobody or nothing that can compare to HIM! Who can love me enough to redeem me and set me up to win before I was even born? We praise HIM because HE is so worthy of it. Can you just begin to tell the LORD all of the things you are thankful for? When you look back over your life at the good and the bad, can you see GOD in the midst of it all? How HE brought

PRAISE

you out again and again. His mercies are new every morning, and the LORD knows we need it. "It is of the LORD's mercies that we are not consumed, because His compassion fails not. They are new every morning: great is THY faithfulness" (Lamentations 3:22–23).

He shall supply all your need (Philippians 4:19). The LORD is a keeper of His word, and HE will never leave us nor forsake us (Hebrews 13:5). We can trust HIM 100 percent above anything or anybody. HE *never* fails! We can *always* depend on HIM knowing that His character is flawless and pure. HE Always wants and knows the best for us and will do it!

"But ye are a chosen generation, a royal priesthood, a holy nation, a peculiar people; that ye should shew forth the praises of HIM who hath called you out of darkness into HIS marvelous light" (1 Peter 2:9).

Will you take the time and from your heart, just tell HIM how you feel about HIM? Begin to meditate on HIM and how Great HE is. HE loves you and you are the apple of HIS eye. HE loves you just where you are. It's not about being perfect or working to get His love, He just loves you...

What are some hinderances
to praise and worship?

Unbelief, guilt/shame, condemnation, fear, hopelessness/weariness, excuses, unforgiveness/issues of the heart, distraction/unfocused, stubbornness, pride, unsubmitted/un-surrendered, unthankful/ungrateful, murmuring/complaining, disobedience/rebellion, complacency/familiarity, unteachable, lack of unity stuck in same cycle/religiosity, spectatorship, lack of fire, lack of understanding.

What should my position and posture be?

I know that my attitude and disposition should be one of thankfulness and gratefulness when I come together to worship the Lord. That I use this opportunity to unite with my brothers and sisters to express love and adoration to our Almighty God. I humbly submit to the guidance of the Holy Spirit and surrender to the will of the Father. I know

I may begin to cry and repent, and I'm not concerned about who's looking at me. This is a good place; a place of sweet communion. I bow in the presence of YOUR sovereign majesty, LORD JESUS!

"Because THY lovingkindness is better than life, my lips shall praise THEE" (Psalm 63:3).

Sound

I just wanted to take a few minutes to talk about sound. Where does sound end and begin? There are no limits to sound. It goes out into the stratosphere. It goes into your future. When we give GOD an explosive unified praise, it douses the pews, goes out the window and down the streets, influences the neighborhood, and infiltrates the atmosphere. We know that our praise rides the waves of air to heaven to the ears of GOD and HE hears, and HE responds.

There are different sounds associated with different things and functions. There's a sound of war, laughter, anger, joy, etc. We just need to know the right sound that the LORD is requesting. There's an action or response associated with the sound produced and an atmospheric influence. There are frequencies and vibrations infused in sound.

As we praise and worship the LORD, not only are words coming out of our mouths but also sound. "So shall My word be that goeth forth out of My mouth: it shall not return unto ME void, but it shall accomplish that which I please, and it shall prosper in the thing whereto I sent it" (Isaiah 55:11). The FATHER set the example of the spoken word and what it can do.

What's in sound, with or without words?

Energy (vibration, frequency, rhythm)
Breath (air)
Force
Tonality (pitch, intonation, modulation)
Resonance (strength, tone color, stress, cadence, accentuation)
Life and death (Proverbs 18:21)
Attitude (expression)
Motive/Intent

PRAISE

We may have favorite artists that assist us in our praise and worship because the sound he/she emits, taps into the place where we are seated. Today we have gospel, country gospel, jazz gospel, rap gospel, etc. that adheres more to our style preference and age. Please don't get me wrong, I'm not saying there are not talented and anointed singers and musicians. But what I am saying is that the style is not directly praise, it is just a musical preference that is a conduit to help me personally engage in praise. What if you can't hear your favorite song, musician or singer? Can you still praise HIM? Understand they are just a conduit to get you to where the HOLY SPIRIT wants to take you.

By the time we ascend in praise to a place of worship, there will be a new sound; the sound that's been orchestrated by the HOLY SPIRIT. A sound that cannot be imitated or duplicated! In many of our places of worship we never make it to that place of intimacy because of time restraints or we may think that there's nothing else left to do. It is the sound of majestic worship that makes the

THE HEART OF GOD TRUE WORSHIP

FATHER stand and take notice of HIS people pursuing HIM with ardent love.

The walls of Jericho came tumbling down! It was the sound of the people and the sound of the trumpets working in concert in obedience to the plan of GOD.

Joshua 6:20,

> So the people shouted when the priests blew the trumpets: and it came to pass when the people heard the sound of the trumpet, and the people shouted with a great shout, that the wall fell down flat, so that the people went up into the city, every man straight before him, and they took the city.

There is a sound associated with the acts and responses of GOD; an atmospheric aroma,

PRAISE

impeding presence of the Kingdom of God. Acts 2:1–2,

> And when the day of Pentecost was fully come, they were all with one accord, in one place. And suddenly there came a sound from heaven as of a rushing mighty wind, and it filled all the house where they were sitting.

Sound can cause molecules to move and objects to break and vibrate predicated on the vibrational frequency of that sound. There was a commercial on TV where singer Ella Fitzgerald hits this high note, and it caused the glass to break. We have dog whistles that cannot be heard by human ears, but by a dog because it's on the dog's frequency. To everything that exist, there is a vibrational frequency sound that can cause a response. The Bible talks about everything being held

THE HEART OF GOD TRUE WORSHIP

together by GOD's divine order and will. Colossians 1: 16–17,

> For by HIM (JESUS) were all things created, that are in heaven, and that are in earth, visible and invisible, whether they be thrones, or dominions, or principalities, or powers: all things were created by HIM, and for HIM: and HE is before all things, and by HIM all things consist.

The LORD holds everything together in its place by HIS preeminent power and purpose.

Sound has energy and force, as well as objective. Sound can create a mood. (You remember those love songs.)

I am taking this time to reiterate the power that comes from unified praise and

PRAISE

worship and the effects of what sound can have. First Samuel 16:23,

> And when it came to pass, when the evil spirit from GOD was upon Saul, that David took a harp, and played with his hand: so Saul was refreshed, and was well, and the evil spirit departed from him.

The Scripture did not say that David sang, but played the harp, and the sound of his playing brought deliverance and refreshing to King Saul.

Second Chronicles 5:13–14,

> It came to pass, as the trumpeters and singers were as *one*, to make *one sound* to be heard in praising and thanking the LORD; and when they lifted up their voice with the trumpets and cymbals and instruments of

> music, and praised the LORD, saying, For HE is good; for HIS mercy endureth for ever: that then the house was filled with a cloud, even the house of the LORD; so that the priest could not stand to minister by reason of the cloud: for the glory of the LORD had filled the house of GOD.

Wow! What an *awesome* experience to have the glory of the LORD arrest you, whereas you couldn't move even if you wanted to. Arrest me! The thought of praising and worshiping the LORD on one accord in one place and the effects of it is so exciting! I can't wait to see what happens the next time we get together to worship HIM.

Worship

Worship, according to the *Webster II New Riverside University Dictionary* means to bow down, prostrate oneself, a posture indicting reverence. The concept of worship is expressed by the term serve or services. A reverent love and allegiance accorded a deity. A set of religious forms, ceremonies, or prayers by which this love is expressed; ardent devotion and love accorded a deity. Bowing as a sign of humility and respect.

Proskuneo (Gk) worship: to kiss like a dog licking his master's hand, reverence, kneeling, or prostrate to do homage, adore (love and respect).

Ascended praise is the gateway to another level of worship. The Bible says to enter into His gates with thanksgiving and into His courts with praise, and we're to be thankful and bless His name. That Scripture implies a progression. We move from the outer court, to the inner court, to the holy of holies (using this analogy).

We don't stay in the outer court but as we progress in praise, we are dying more and more to self as we pursue a divine encounter with the LORD. I look at ascending in praise like an airplane that is at a gate and picks up its passengers and begin to move down the runway and begins to ascend until it reaches its designated altitude. We were never meant to stay at the gate but move to the ultimate place the LORD would have us to be.

The Levites (worshippers) and the priests were taught how to go in before the LORD, and the people followed their lead. Everything was done with reverence and carefulness according to the divine order of GOD.

If you do not praise and worship GOD, you will be dry and barren. Praise and worship replenishes, nourishes, revives, empowers, and positions us to receive from the LORD. GOD's desire is to commune with His children and to bless them. There is no *greater* love than the love HE has for us. We will gladly show our love and appreciation in heart felt worship.

I have noticed a difference in the sound and activity when it comes to praise and worship. When we praise (even though praise is a part of worship) there is more movement, activity, noise, exclamations, celebration, and exuberance over what HE has done, is doing, and will do. As we ascend in praise, there begins to be a type of metamorphosis that changes the sound as well as the impression in the atmosphere. In worship, the sound is more subtle, reverent, if any sound. There's less movement in reverence to HIS presence, stillness, weeping, bowing, and laying prostrate.

I am not saying that this is what happens every time because this is based on what GOD wants, HIS will, and HIS purpose. We're yielded temples of worship. "What? Know ye not that your body is the temple of the HOLY GHOST which is in you, which ye have of GOD, ye are not your own?" (1 Corinthians 6:19). We're to present our bodies as a living sacrifice (Romans 12:1). Yielded worship will

THE HEART OF GOD TRUE WORSHIP

cause these temples to be filled with the light of His glory.

Worship can be expressed in many ways; in our service, praise, obedience, giving, prayers, various ceremonies, and ritual forms. I want to go a little further and say that worship is more than rituals and ceremonies and the methods by which they are demonstrated, but it is relational and not just functional.

In Genesis (3:8–9), when God asked Adam, "Where art thou?" He was not just talking about naturally, physically asking, *Adam, where is your location, but I submit to you, it was relationally, spiritually. You're not in the place you are supposed to be. There has been a violation of our relationship; a breach. We know each other, Adam.* Obedience, like giving is a part of our worship, but obedience, void of love and honor, is not acceptable worship. I know I may get in trouble for saying that, but you can obey something or someone and not love or respect it. Beloved, remember, we are talking about what is acceptable to God, and not man.

Worship is about what's in our hearts. It's our attitude and position towards God. King

WORSHIP

David said, "When THOU saidst, seek ye MY face; my heart said unto THEE, THY face, LORD will I seek" (Psalm 27:8). There is a conscious awareness of who GOD is. GOD is not separate from what HE does, have done, or will do; HE does because HE is. Worship is not predicated on what HE's done because if HE never pays another light bill, heal my body, or restore my marriage, HE will eternally still be GOD! Who HE is will infinitely be infallible, sovereign, absolute, and supreme!

Revelation 4:10–11,

> The four and twenty elders fall down before HIM that sat on the throne, and worship HIM that liveth for ever and ever, and cast down their crowns before the throne, saying, THOU art worthy, O LORD, to receive glory and honor and power: for THOU hast created all things, and for THY pleasure they are and were created.

THE HEART OF GOD TRUE WORSHIP

The four and twenty elders cast down their crowns as though they meant nothing to them and fell down before the All-deserving KING and worshipped HIM! The elders did not consider it demeaning or belittling to them to do this act of worship. But I dare say they considered it an honor and a privilege to give glory and honor to HIM who sat upon the throne.

Worship is a place of intimacy. In that place of worship, sometimes my heart speaks nonaudible words that my mouth can't articulate, and my mind can't grasp, but my spirit expresses. Worship is a matter of the heart. JESUS says, "This people draweth nigh unto ME with their lips; but their heart is far from ME" (Matthew 15:8). HE wants all of us. The greatest commandment is to love; love HIM. We're to love HIM not just in our actions with the fruit of our lips but with our hearts. JESUS said unto them, "Thou shalt love the LORD thy GOD with all of thy heart, and all thy soul, and with all thy mind" (Matthew 22:37). "Blessed are they that keep HIS testimonies and seek HIM with the whole heart." (Psalm 119:2).

WORSHIP

The LORD wants us not to just know of HIM about HIM, but to know HIM. We can learn of and about HIM through other people, coming to church, and hearing and reading the Bible. But to *know* HIM, one must spend time with HIM not only reading HIS word but also in prayer, praise, and worship. It's applied information learned spiritually and naturally that declares the awesomeness of who HE is and empowers us.

There will be times in our lives when we are looking to see or hear from GOD, and it seems like HE is nowhere to be found. And you are wondering if HE even hears you? You feel like if HE doesn't come right now, you're not going to make it. Beloved, in those dire times, you've got to know HIM. That means no matter what things look like or even what has been said, you have to believe in HIM and HIS character.

Trust HIM more than anything or anyone. HE cannot lie, and HE remains the same. "For when GOD made promise to Abraham, because HE could swear by no greater, HE swear by HIMSELF" (Hebrews 6:13). That's how faithful and committed GOD is to HIS

THE HEART OF GOD TRUE WORSHIP

word, both spoken and written. You may not be able to read or have a Bible, but you can still seek to develop a relationship with Him, and He will make a way to provide you with whatever you may need.

Worship is a place of knowing, intimacy, a place of conception. Adam knew Eve (Genesis 4:1). God said to Jeremiah before He formed him in his mother's womb; He knew him (Jeremiah 1:5). That word knew in both of those scriptures have the same meaning. Adam knew Eve, and she conceived. God knew Jeremiah and placed destiny and purpose on the inside of him to be birthed at the appointed time according to His will.

In worship there is an awareness and intentional effort on our part to engage in the process of this intimate relationship with our God. Whatever the Lord has for you to see, know, hear, or do, you will receive it in a place of worship. Everything is easier and clearer in a place of worship. It's easier to hear His voice. Recognize the anointing and know the flow of the Holy Spirit in His presence.

When we pursue a committed relationship with God, there will be evidence that

84

WORSHIP

will be birthed out of that place of intimacy; it will be fruitful. Let me give you an example: A husband and wife can be on opposite sides of a crowded room, and their eyes can meet and know exactly what the other one is saying without speaking a word. Why? Because they are connected. They are one. They know each other. They've spent time together. When we spend time with the LORD, we will develop a *knowing* that will *anchor* us when everything around us is not making any sense and seemingly things are falling apart.

GOD is seeking a people who would worship HIM in spirit and in truth with the understanding of who HE is.

> But the hour cometh and now is when the true worshippers shall worship the FATHER in spirit and in truth: For the FATHER seeketh such to worship HIM. GOD is a spirit: and they that worship HIM must worship HIM in spirit and in truth. (John 4:23–24)

THE HEART OF GOD TRUE WORSHIP

The FATHER is seeking true worshippers. We read earlier that we must believe that HE is, and we must worship HIM in spirit and in truth. Did you read, as I read the word *must*? That means that those things mentioned are a requirement; anything less than that is unacceptable. That suggest that not everything we offer up as worship is acceptable to GOD.

Let's give an example: The offering given by Cain and Abel was a type of worship. Abel's offering was accepted, but Cains' offering was rejected. Let's see what we do know about what was offered up as an offering between these two brothers.

> And in process of time it came to pass, that Cain brought of the fruit of the ground an offering unto the LORD. And Abel, He also brought of the firstlings of his flock and the fat thereof. And the LORD had respect unto Abel and to his offering: but unto Cain and his

WORSHIP

offering He had not respect.
(Genesis 4:3–5a)

We can see that Abel was very conscientious and meticulous about what He offered up to the Lord. Abel took the time to select the best (firstling/fat) and prepared his offering before presenting it unto the Lord. All the Scripture says about Cain's offering is that he brought it before the Lord. So we don't know whether Cain just grabbed whatever fruit, even off the ground, he saw and threw it in his offering basket or what, but we do know it wasn't his best. The Scripture specifically describes Abel's offering and Cain's offering is void of any description at all.

What is said and not said points to the differences in the two brothers' offerings: their worship. We should always want our worship to be acceptable to the Lord. We must diligently worship in faith and in spirit and truth. This is not an option, but what the Father commands. It takes perseverance in order to go pass our feelings in pursuance of His face and not just His hand. We must

THE HEART OF GOD TRUE WORSHIP

begin to allow time for true worship in our services.

The average Christian church consists of two or three services that last no longer than an hour and a half, at the most two hours. What's included in those time slots are announcements, prayer, two praise and two worship songs, preaching, alter call, offering, and the benediction. In most cases, those that come don't get to witness the manifestation of the Kingdom of GOD; only a good feeling and a good word. But there is so much more!

I'm talking about the leading of the HOLY SPIRIT to that GOD ordained place of worship, where the HOLY SPIRIT backs up the word of GOD in extravagant demonstration that saves, heals, delivers, manifest miracles, open blinded eyes, and more. The leaders must be able to identify the move of the HOLY SPIRIT and the anointing. If we want to experience all that GOD has for us when we gather, we must stop trying to fit an unlimited GOD into our limited program!

Do you know that by allowing the demonstration of the HOLY SPIRIT in our services, it's a testimony and witness of the power

WORSHIP

and LORDSHIP of our Savior JESUS CHRIST? I guarantee that if we submit to HIS guidance, we will not be there all night. If we yield, we won't miss out on anything, but gain everything. Let's take the time and submit our services to HIM. HE will do what needs to be done in a timely manner, but we must stop forfeiting the move of GOD for our own personal agenda.

Worship until you become what you do. Worship is who you are. We just don't do worship. Worship is a relationship! My first order in relationships is my relationship with GOD. To imply worship is something we just do suggest that when we're not engaged in the activity of worship, that worship is not present, that it's something you can put on and take off. I'm trying to challenge your mindset to another way to view worship. When you become what you do, it begins to be a part of who you are—your DNA, your personality, a part of the essence of your very being.

You are a vessel of worship, that was created to have relationship with your creator. We don't just have church; we are the church! We go to a building—we call church—where we gather together to worship the only true and Living GOD. We go to fellowship, pray, hear the rhema and logos, and to worship GOD in spirit and in truth to experience the power of heaven.

True worship looks like HIM!

The Glory

When the glory of GOD manifests, everyone will know it without a word being spoken. Glory is preeminently an attribute of GOD or people or things associated with GOD. We see various aspects of HIS glory when we look at HIS marvelous creation. "The heavens declare the glory of GOD: and the firmament sheweth HIS handiwork" (Psalm 19:1). Every place that we look we can see the work of HIS hands. "The glory of the LORD shall endure forever: the LORD shall rejoice in HIS works (Psalm 104:31). What a wonderful thing to be privileged to bask in the beauty of HIS holiness, HIS glory.

GOD is not separate from HIS glory, so when HIS glory comes, that means HE's here. HIS glory does not hit some and miss others. It's just like the sun, the only way everyone

THE HEART OF GOD TRUE WORSHIP

under the sun does not see and experience its brilliance is that it's obscured by something, other than that, it hits everything within its capacity.

When we get to this place in our corporate worship, there's not a lot of movement, if any at all. I would say, the singers aren't singing, and the musicians aren't playing because of the reverence and awe of GOD in the place. In many cases, we've been taught to keep playing and singing, but we must learn to be sensitive and honor and respect the presence of GOD.

> It came to pass, as the trumpeters and singers were as one, to make one sound to be heard in praising and thanking the LORD; and when they lifted up their voice with the trumpets and cymbals and instruments of music, and praised the LORD saying, For HE is good; for HIS mercy endureth for ever: that then the house was

THE GLORY

> filled with a cloud, even the house of the LORD; so that the priests could not stand to minister by reason of the cloud: for the glory of the LORD had filled the house of GOD. (2 Chronicles 5: 13–14)

The kabod (Heb) (splendor, honor, weight) of HIS glory. The literal weight of HIS glory will cause you to bow, to lay prostrate. In this place, HIS presence will make you not want to even move! You just want to stay there and soak and bask in HIS presence. Moses asked GOD to see HIS glory. "And it shall come to pass, while MY glory passeth by, that I will put thee in a clift of the rock, and will cover thee with MY hand while I pass by" (Exodus 33:22). You can read in Exodus 34:29–35, where Moses face shinned/glowed so much so that he put a veil over it.

It was evident to all that Moses had been in the presence of the Almighty GOD. No one has to say a word, but we will be changed without prayers or hands being laid. We will

THE HEART OF GOD TRUE WORSHIP

be transformed! When the glory of GOD manifests, it will be apparent to all that's present. The King of glory is here!

> Lift up your heads, O ye gates; and be ye lift up, ye everlasting doors; and the King of glory shall come in. Who is this King of glory? The LORD strong and mighty; the LORD mighty in battle. Lift up your heads, O ye gates; even lift them up, ye everlasting doors; and the King of glory shall come. Who is this King of glory? The LORD of hosts, HE is the King of glory. (Psalm 24:7–10)

Oh, the awesomeness of our sovereign GOD! "Heaven is MY throne, and earth is MY footstool" (Acts 7:49). Where can we go that we don't see the throne of GOD? Just how big is our GOD? "Whither shall I go from THY spirit? Or wither shall I flee from THY presence? If I ascend up into heaven, THOU art there: if I make my bed in hell, behold, THOU art there" (Psalm 139:7–8). King Solomon said, "The heaven and heaven of heavens cannot contain THEE" (1 Kings 8:27b). Sometimes, I sit and think about GOD and how great HE is. My mind can't conceive the vastness of HIS excellency, HIS holiness and HIS never-ending love. How can such a magnificent GOD be so personable yet absolute sovereignty?

HIS grace is sufficient, and HIS mercy is everlasting. "Great is the LORD, and HIS greatness is unsearchable" (Psalm 145:3). HE set us up to win. HE thought about us before we ever thought about HIM. HE deserves our extravagant praise, our worship; HE's so worthy. Whatever we need is found in HIM. We need HIM; HE is our breath of life, the very air that we breath. "Bless the LORD, O my soul and all that is within me, bless HIS holy name. Bless the LORD, O my soul, and forget not all HIS benefits" (Psalm 103:1–2).

THE HEART OF GOD TRUE WORSHIP

Some things you may experience but not limited to:

Weeping
Lay prostrate/ rocking
Warmth/heat
Stillness/Awe
Feeling a weightiness/Exhaustion
Peace/comfort/love/forgiveness
See Angels
See Cloudiness/Smokiness
See Light/Glistening/colors
Revelation/Prophetic
Impartation

LORD, I will set aside time to spend with YOU, so that I may grow in my relationship with YOU. YOU are my substance, O GOD. Without you, I have no life. There is no one greater than YOU—supreme, holy, and true. I will worship YOU in spirit and in truth. My praise shall go before me. Blessed is the name of the LORD from everlasting to everlasting. Let YOUR name be exalted, LORD JESUS! Amen!

Decree and Declaration

Thou shalt also decree a thing and it shall be established unto thee and the light shall shine upon thy ways.

—Job 22:28

*D*ecree: An order usually having the force of law; a religious ordinance enacted by council or titular head; foreordaining will; a judicial decision.

Declare: To make known formally, officially, or explicitly; to state clearly and strongly.

I decree and declare that everyone who reads this book that the eyes of their understanding will be enlightened. That their relationship with You, Lord, will grow exponentially. I decree and declare that they will walk in a deeper revelatory understanding and knowledge of their call and divine purpose. That everything within them is rightly aligned with YOUR purpose and will, and everything that YOU have ordained to be in their lives at this appointed time will manifest, no delay! I decree and declare that their spiritual discernment increases and the awareness of the HOLY SPIRIT living on the inside and the LORDSHIP of JESUS CHRIST be personified.

I thank YOU, LORD, for being their covering, keeper, and shield. I thank YOU, LORD, for the HOLY SPIRIT, guiding each one into all truth and manifesting the kingdom of GOD in their lives. I thank YOU, LORD, for helping each one to be faithful over every assignment YOU have given them. I praise YOU, LORD, for great is THY faithfulness and love towards YOUR children. In the name of JESUS, it is so, and at the appointed time, so shall it manifest. Glory!

Glossary

Limited Glossary

Barak (Heb): to bless, to kneel, to adore, to praise, to salute.

"I will bless the LORD at all times: HIS praise shall continually be in my mouth" (Psalm 34:1).

Halal (Heb): to be clear, to shine, to make a boast; and thus, to be clamorously foolish; to rave; to celebrate; make a boast, sing praise, be worthy of praise, rage, renowned, shine.

"Ye that fear the LORD, praise HIM; all ye the seed of Jacob, glorify HIM; and fear HIM, all ye the see of Israel" (Psalm 22:23).

Zamar (Heb): properly to touch the strings or parts of a musical instrument, i.e., play upon it; to make music, accompanied

THE HEART OF GOD TRUE WORSHIP

by the voice; hence to celebrate in song and music: give praise, sing forth praises, psalms.

"Sing unto the LORD with thanksgiving; sing praise upon the harp unto our GOD" (Psalm 147:7).

Tehilla (Heb): laudation, a hymn, praise.

"Enter into HIS gates with thanksgiving, and into HIS courts with praise: be thankful unto HIM, and bless HIS name" (Psalm 100:4).

Shabach (Heb): properly to address in a loud tone, commend, glory, keep in, praise, still, triumph

"One generation shall praise THY works to another and shall declare THY mighty acts" (Psalm 145:4).

Towdah (Heb): properly an extension of the hand, adoration, confession, praise, sacrifice of praise, thanks, thanksgiving, thank offering.

"Lift up your hands in the sanctuary and bless the LORD" (Psalm 134:2).

Yada (Heb): literally to hold out the hand, physically to throw at or away; especially to revere or worship (with extended

100

GLOSSARY

hands); intensively bemoan (by wringing of hands), cast, cast out, confess, make a confession, praise, shoot, thanks, give thanks, be thankful, thanksgiving.

"Thus, will I bless THEE while I live: I will lift up my hands in THY name" (Psalm 63:4).

Hosanna (Gk): save, rescue, savior.

"And the multitudes that went before, and that followed, cried, saying, Hosanna to the SON of David: Blessed is HE that cometh in the name of the LORD; Hosanna in the highest" (Matthew 21:9).

Alleluia (Gk): Praise Yah Hallelujah: Praise the LORD; to praise.

"And the four and twenty elders and the four beasts fell down and worshipped GOD that sat on the throne, saying, Amen; Alleluia" (Revelation 19:4).

Doxa (Gk): glory, honor, praise, worship.

"Glory to GOD in the highest, and on earth peace, good will toward men" (Luke 2:14).

Theosebes (Gk): properly reverence (toward GOD); true piety shown by devout wor-

THE HEART OF GOD TRUE WORSHIP

shippers, i.e. God fearing people who venerate the things of God.

"Now we know that God heareth not sinners: but if any man be a worshipper of God, and doeth His will, him He heareth" (John 9:31).

Espainos (Gk): laudation; concretely a commendable thing: praise.

"Which is the earnest of our inheritance until the redemption of the purchased possession, unto the praise of His glory" (Ephesians 1:14).

Chairo (Gk): to rejoice, be glad, to rejoice exceedingly, to be well, thrive, salutations, hail

"Rejoice in the Lord always: and again, I say, Rejoice" (Philippians 4:4).

Hallomai (Gk): to leap, to spring up, gush up.

"And He leaping up stood, and walked, and entered with them into the temple, walking, and leaping, and praising God" (Acts 3:8).

Ado (Gk): to the praise of anyone, to sing.

"Speaking to yourselves in psalms and hymns and spiritual songs, singing and

GLOSSARY

making melody in your heart to the LORD" (Ephesians 5:19).

Names of GOD

Elohim: (plural) GODs, angels, exceeding, GOD, GODdess, Godly, great, very great, judges, mighty.

"In the beginning GOD (Elohim) created the heaven and the earth" (Genesis 1:1).

YHWH: GOD.

"Thrice in the year shall all your men children appear before the LORD GOD, the GOD of Israel" (Exodus 34:23).

YAWEH: GOD, JEHOVAH, LORD.

"And GOD spoke to Moses, and said unto him, I am the LORD" (Exodus 6:2).

JEHOVAH: GOD, LORD.

"And I appeared unto Abraham, unto Isaac, and unto Jacob, by the name of GOD Almighty, but by MY name JEHOVAH was I not known to them" (Exodus 6:3).

Adonai: Hebrew name for GOD, LORD; Adon (singular) Adonai (plural) LORD of LORDS.

THE HEART OF GOD TRUE WORSHIP

"For, the LORD your GOD is GOD of GODS, and LORD of LORDS, a great GOD, a mighty, and terrible, which regardeth not persons, nor taketh reward" (Deuteronomy 10:17).

JEHOVAH Shalom: The LORD our peace.

"And the LORD said unto him, Peace be unto thee; fear not: thou shalt not die. 24) Then Gideon built an alter there unto the LORD, and called it JEHOVAH-shalom: unto this day it is yet in Ophrah of the Abiezrites" (Judges 6:23–24).

JEHOVAH Jireh: The LORD will provide.

"And Abraham lifted up his eyes, and looked, and behold behind him a ram caught in a thicket by his horns: and Abraham went and took the ram, and offered him up for a burnt offering in the stead of his SON. And Abraham called the name of that place JEHOVAH-jireh: as it is said to this day, In the mount of the LORD it shall be seen" (Genesis 22:13–14).

"But my GOD shall supply all your need according to HIS riches in glory by CHRIST JESUS" (Philippians 4:19).

GLOSSARY

JEHOVAH Rapha: The LORD who heals.

"Who forgiveth all thine iniquities; who health all thy diseases" (Psalm 103:3).

JEHOVAH Roi: The LORD my shepherd.

"The LORD is my shepherd; I shall not want" (Psalm 23:1).

JEHOVAH Shammah: The LORD is there (here).

"It was round about eighteen thousand measures: and the name of the city from that day shall be, The LORD is there" (Ezekiel 48:35).

JEHOVAH Nissi: The LORD is our banner.

"And the LORD said unto Moses, 'Write this for a memorial in a book, ad rehearse it in the ears of Joshua: for I will utterly put out the remembrance of Amelek from under heaven. And Moses built an altar, and called the name of it JEHOVAH-nissi'" (Exodus 17:14–15).

JEHOVAH Mekaddishkem (Mekadesh): The LORD who sanctifies.

"And the LORD spoke unto Moses, saying, 'Speak thou also unto the children of Israel, saying, Verily MY sabbaths ye shall keep for it is a sign between ME and you throughout your generations; that ye

THE HEART OF GOD TRUE WORSHIP

may know I am the LORD that doth sanctify you'" (Exodus 31:12–13).

JEHOVAH Tsidkenu: The LORD our righteousness.

"Behold, the days come, saith the LORD, that I will raise unto David a righteous Branch, and a King shall reign and prosper, and shall execute judgement and justice in the earth. In HIS days Judah shall be saved, and Israel shall dwell safely: and this is HIS name whereby HE shall be called, THE LORD OUR RIGHTEOUSNESS" (Jeremiah 23:5–6).

JEHOVAH Sabaoth: The LORD of Hosts (armies).

"Behold, the hire of the laborers who have reaped down your fields, which is of you kept back by fraud, crieth: and the cries of them which have reaped are entered into the ears of the LORD Sabaoth" (James 5:4).

JESUS (JESHUAH): Salvation, Deliverance, Prosperity, Victory.

"The Spirit of the LORD GOD is upon ME to preach good tidings unto the meek; HE hath sent ME to bind up the broken

GLOSSARY

hearted, to proclaim liberty to the captives, and the opening of the prison to them that are bound; To proclaim the acceptable year of the LORD" (Isaiah 61:1–2).

JESUS said, "The Spirit of the LORD is upon ME, because HE hath anointed ME to preach the gospel to the poor; HE hath sent ME to heal the brokenhearted, to preach deliverance to the captives, and recovering of sight to the blind, to set at liberty them that are bruised, 19) to preach the acceptable year of the LORD" (Luke 4:18–19).

CHRIST: Anointed.

"And it shall come to pass in that day, that his burden shall be taken away from off thy shoulder, and his yoke from off thy neck, and the yoke shall be destroyed because of the anointing" (Isaiah 10:27).

JESUS is called:

Lamb of GOD: "The next day John seeth JESUS coming unto him, and saith, Behold the

THE HEART OF GOD TRUE WORSHIP

Lamb of God, which taketh away the sin of the world" (John1:29).

Rock: "And did all drink the same spiritual drink: for they drank of that spiritual Rock that followed them: and that Rock was Christ" (1 Corinthians 10:4).

High Priest: "Whither the forerunner is for us entered, even Jesus, made an high priest for ever after the order of Melchisedec" (Hebrews 6:20).

Head of the Church: "For the husband is the head of the wife, even as Christ is the head of the church: and He is the savior of the body" (Ephesians 5:23).

Bread of Life: "And Jesus said unto them, I am the bread of life: he that cometh to me shall never hunger; and He that believeth on me shall never thirst" (John 6:35).

Redeemer: "For I know that my redeemer liveth, and that He shall stand at the latter day upon the earth" (Job 19:25).

Bridegroom: "And Jesus said unto them, can the children of the bridechamber mourn, as long as the bridegroom is with them? But the days will come, when the bride-

GLOSSARY

groom shall be taken from them, and then shall they fast" (Matthew 9:15).

Alpha and Omega: "I am Alpha and Omega, the beginning and the end, the first and the last" (Revelation 22: 13).

King of kings and Lord of lords: "Which in His times He shall shew, who is the blessed and only Potentate, the King of kings, and the Lord of Lords" (1 Timothy 6:15).

Resurrection and the Life: Jesus said unto her, "I am the resurrection, and the life: He that believeth in Me, though He were dead, yet shall He live" (John 11:25).

Lion of the Tribe of Judah: "And one of the elders saith unto me, Weep not: behold, the Lion of the tribe of Juda, the Root of David, hath prevailed to open the book, and to lose the seven seals thereof" (Revelation 5:5).

Holy One: "Saying, Let us alone; what have we to do with Thee, Thou Jesus of Nazareth? art Thou come to destroy us? I know Thee who Thou art, the Holy One of God" (Mark 1:24).

THE HEART OF GOD TRUE WORSHIP

Image of the Invisible GOD: "In whom we have redemption through HIS blood, even the forgiveness of sins: 15) Who is the image of the invisible GOD, the firstborn of every creature" (Colossians 1:14–15).

Only Begotten SON: "For GOD so loved the world, that HE gave HIS only begotten SON, that whosoever believeth in HIM should not perish, but have everlasting life" (John 3:16).

Mediator: "For there is one GOD, and one mediator between GOD and men, the man CHRIST JESUS" (I Timothy 2:5).

Author and Finisher of Our Faith: "Looking unto JESUS the author and finisher of our faith; who for the joy that was set before HIM endured the cross, despising the shame, and is set down at the right hand of the throne of GOD" (Hebrews 12:2).

The Way, the Truth, and the Life: JESUS saith unto him, "I am the way, the truth, and the life: no man cometh unto the FATHER, but by ME" (John 14:6).

Bright and Morning Star: "I JESUS have sent mine angel to testify unto you these things in the churches. I am the root and

GLOSSARY

the offspring of David, and the bright and morning star" (Revelation 22:16).

Savior: "And said unto the woman, now we believe, not because of thy saying: for we have heard HIM ourselves, and know that this is indeed the CHRIST, the Savior of the world" (John 4:42).

Emmanuel: "Behold, a virgin shall be with child, and shall bring forth a SON, and they shall call HIS name Emmanuel, which being interpreted is, GOD with us" (Matthew 1:23).

Messiah: "He first findeth his own brother Simon, and saith unto him, we have found the Messias, which is, being interpreted, the CHRIST" (John 1:41).

Beloved SON: "And lo a voice from heaven, saying, 'This is MY beloved SON, in whom I am well pleased'" (Matthew 3:17).

Wonderful Counsellor, Prince of Peace: "For unto us a child is born, unto us a SON is given: and the government shall be upon HIS shoulder: and HIS name shall be called Wonderful, Counsellor, The

THE HEART OF GOD TRUE WORSHIP

mighty GOD, The everlasting FATHER, The Prince of Peace" (Isaiah 9:6).

Teacher: "The same came to JESUS by night, and said unto HIM, Rabbi, we know that THOU art a teacher come from GOD: for no man can do these miracles that THOU doest, except GOD be with HIM" (John 3:2).

The Door: JESUS said, "I am the door: by ME if any man enters in, he shall be saved, and shall go in and out, and find pasture" (John 10:9).

About the Author

D r. Laurita Bledsoe is an ordained minister and founder of GOD's Anointed Ministry, SWIM and The Legacy 7 LLC. She is a mother, grandmother, and great-grandmother and considers that to be one of GOD's great blessings to her. She has co-labored with many ministries of various denominations and organizations to empower individuals, families, communities, and regions, demonstrating the Kingdom of GOD. Her motto is to use every gift, talent, ability, skill, and resource to advance the Kingdom of GOD on earth through these earthen vessels in the name of Yeshua!

Her book, *The Heart of GOD True Worship,* is one of the vehicles by which those that read it will begin to operate in another dimension of worship and relationship with the FATHER. This book is much needed to help us understand the power that comes from unified purposeful worship.